Concise Encyclopedia of Preaching

Also published by Westminster John Knox Press

ENCYCLOPEDIA OF THE REFORMED FAITH
edited by Donald K. McKim

THE WESTMINSTER DICTIONARY OF CHRISTIAN ETHICS
edited by James F. Childress and John Macquarrie

THE WESTMINSTER DICTIONARY OF CHRISTIAN SPIRITUALITY
edited by Gordon S. Wakefield

THE WESTMINSTER DICTIONARY OF CHRISTIAN THEOLOGY
edited by Alan Richardson and John Bowden

THE WESTMINSTER DICTIONARY OF CHURCH HISTORY
edited by Jerald C. Brauer

THE NEW WESTMINSTER DICTIONARY OF LITURGY AND WORSHIP
edited by J. G. Davies

THE NEW WESTMINSTER DICTIONARY OF THE BIBLE
edited by Henry Snyder Gehman

Concise Encyclopedia of Preaching

WILLIAM H. WILLIMON
RICHARD LISCHER
editors

Westminster John Knox Press
Louisville, Kentucky

Book design by Publishers' WorkGroup
Cover design by Tanya R. Hahn

First edition

Published by Westminster John Knox Press
Louisville, Kentucky

This book is printed on acid-free paper that meets the American National Standards Institute Z39.48 standard. ∞

PRINTED IN THE UNITED STATES OF AMERICA

00 01 02 03 04 — 10 9 8 7 6 5 4 3

Library of Congress Cataloging-in-Publication Data

Concise encyclopedia of preaching / William H. Willimon,
Richard Lischer, editors. — 1st ed.
       p.   cm.
    ISBN 0-664-21942-X (alk. paper)
    1. Preaching—Encyclopedias.   2. Clergy—Biography—Dictionaries.
I. Willimon, William H.   II. Lischer, Richard.
BV4211.2.C583   1995
251'.003—dc20   94–3469

To Our Students

How are they to hear without a preacher?

—Romans 10:14

Preface

We have created the *Concise Encyclopedia of Preaching* as a labor of love for the church's great tradition of preaching. Only after we became deeply involved in the work did we realize how rich and varied that tradition is. It ranges from theological reflection on the meaning of authority in the pulpit to the twinge of anxiety experienced by every preacher who stands to speak. That tradition is as old as the prophets and as modern (or post-modern) as the latest theories of communication. It is as familiar as current resources and as unfamiliar (at least to North Americans) as Scandinavian or Asian developments in homiletics.

Essentially, the book consists of three types of entries: (1) historical, critical, and theological essays on a wide variety of topics related to preaching; (2) practical directions for the production and delivery of sermons; and (3) biographical studies of individuals whose work has deeply influenced the church and its proclamation. Although this is not a book of sermons or sermon ideas, we have supplemented the biographical articles with brief excerpts from sermons that are representative of important preachers or movements in homiletics. The reader will see at once that the most difficult part of the editorial process was the selection of individual persons for study. The encyclopedia was to be "concise," which means that many significant preachers and thinkers have been omitted. We have tried to choose those persons (1) who were (or are) exemplary preachers, or (2) who were in some way formative for the discipline of homiletics, or (3) who put the stamp of their faithfulness or genius on their generation and, in some cases, upon succeeding generations. Just as we have tried to give "voices" to some preachers by means of the sermon excerpts, so we have also included studies of women and minorities whose voices have not been heeded or appreciated by the dominant culture.

We hope this book will find users among practicing preachers, as well as among academic students of preaching. The former should find refreshment of what they may already know; the latter, instruction and a place to begin their reflection or preaching.

For those who wish to read the *Encyclopedia* systematically according to a field of interest, let us suggest several tracks. In each track, the articles should be read in the following order:

Theology

Theology of Preaching
Word of God
Hermeneutics
Proclamation
Doctrine
Authority
Reason

Homiletics

Homily
Homiletics: Teaching of
Pedagogy of Preaching
History of Preaching
Homiletics and Preaching—
    in Africa
    in Asia
    in German-Speaking Europe
    in India
    in Latin America
    in North America
    in Scandinavia

Many other topics could be included, and the reader may construct his or her own program of study. Considerable overlap exists between tracks, but the multiplicity of perspectives and redundancy of topics also contribute to the richness of the book. Likewise, our many authors cannot possibly represent a single perspective on preaching or a school of homiletics, but we believe this variety also constitutes a strength of the *Encyclopedia*. An asterisk (*) beside a word in an article directs the reader's attention to an article on a related subject elsewhere in the book.

We owe many people our thanks for their help on this book. Early in its development, several scholars in the field of homiletics suggested topics and persons for inclusion. We were fortunate to consult with Elizabeth Achtemeier, O. C. Edwards, Jr., Walter Burghardt, S. J., Thomas Long, James Cox, James Earl Massey, Carol Norén, and Joan Delaplane, O. P. Charles Campbell helped with research in the early stages. Many colleagues—too many to mention—put us

on the trail of specialists and appropriate authors for various articles. Finding the right person to write each of the two hundred articles was a bit like detective work. By far the most pleasurable aspect of our work—over and above our own friendship—has been the many contacts and conversations with our authors, especially those we had not known before. These conversations have enriched not only the *Encyclopedia* but also our personal and professional lives.

Finally, we wish to express our thanks to Cynthia Thompson of Westminster John Knox Press for her persistence and editorial guidance; to Jackie Andrews of Duke University Chapel, who helped with the excerpts and permissions to reprint them; and Gail Chappell of Duke Divinity School, who organized our files and prepared the entire manuscript for publication.

Anyone foolish enough to prepare a dictionary or an encyclopedia gives too many hostages to fortune. The possibilities for small errors of fact and large errors of perspective, to say nothing of egregious sins of omission, are endless. Thus we offer this resource to the church's preachers with humility—and with the words of Dr. Johnson who, when asked to explain the errors in his recently published *Dictionary of the English Language*, replied, "Ignorance, Madam, pure ignorance."

WILLIAM WILLIMON
RICHARD LISCHER
Durham, North Carolina

Contributors

Elizabeth Achtemeier
Union Theological Seminary in Virginia
Richmond, Virginia

P. Mark Achtemeier
University of Dubuque Theological
  Seminary
Dubuque, Iowa

Ronald J. Allen
Christian Theological Seminary
Indianapolis, Indiana

John R. Archer
Oakland, California

Mary Christine Athans, B.V.M.
The School of Divinity
The Saint Paul Seminary
University of St. Thomas
St. Paul, Minnesota

David W. Augsburger
Fuller Theological Seminary
Pasadena, California

Raymond Bailey
Southern Baptist Theological Seminary
Louisville, Kentucky

David L. Bartlett
Yale University Divinity School
New Haven, Connecticut

Charles L. Bartow
Princeton Theological Seminary
Princeton, New Jersey

Barbara Bate
General Board of Discipleship
The United Methodist Church
Nashville, Tennessee

Peter Bayley
Gonville and Caius College
Cambridge University
Cambridge, England

Perry H. Biddle
Nashville, Tennessee

Michael W. Blastic, O.F.M. Conv.
Washington Theological Union
Silver Spring, Maryland

Walter R. Bouman
Trinity Lutheran Seminary
Columbus, Ohio

Carl E. Braaten
Center for Catholic and Evangelical
  Theology
Northfield, Minnesota

Walter Brueggemann
Columbia Theological Seminary
Decatur, Georgia

Walter J. Burghardt, S.J.
Woodstock Theological Center
Annapolis, Maryland

John Burke, O.P.
Dominican House of Studies
Washington, D.C.

David Buttrick
Vanderbilt University Divinity School
Nashville, Tennessee

Charles L. Campbell
Columbia Theological Seminary
Decatur, Georgia

Ted A. Campbell
Wesley Theological Seminary
Washington, D.C.

William J. Carl, III
The First Presbyterian Church
Dallas, Texas

Jackson W. Carroll
Duke University Divinity School
Durham, North Carolina

Donald F. Chatfield
Garrett-Evangelical Theological
   Seminary
Evanston, Illinois

Jana Childers
San Francisco Theological Seminary
San Anselmo, California

William Sloane Coffin, Jr.
Strafford, Vermont

John W. Cook
The Henry Luce Foundation
New York, New York

James W. Cox
Southern Baptist Theological Seminary
Louisville, Kentucky

Fred B. Craddock
Candler School of Theology
Emory University
Atlanta, Georgia

James L. Crenshaw
Duke University Divinity School
Durham, North Carolina

Mitties McDonald DeChamplain
Fuller Theological Seminary
Pasadena, California

Joan Delaplane, O.P.
Aquinas Institute of Theology
St. Louis, Missouri

Donald E. Demaray
Asbury Theological Seminary
Wilmore, Kentucky

Dawn De Vries
McCormick Theological Seminary
Chicago, Illinois

Jon T. Diefenthaler
Bethany Lutheran Church
Waynesboro, Virginia

Arlo D. Duba
University of Dubuque Theological
   Seminary
Dubuque, Iowa

Patty Ann T. Earle
Messiah Episcopal Church
Mayodan, North Carolina

O. C. Edwards, Jr.
College of Preachers
Washington, D.C.

Mark Ellingsen
Interdenominational Theological Center
Atlanta, Georgia

Richard L. Eslinger
Trinity United Methodist Church
Niles, Michigan

Gillian R. Evans
Fitzwilliam College
Cambridge University
Cambridge, England

Clyde E. Fant
The Chapel
Stetson University
DeLand, Florida

Al Fasol
Southwestern Baptist Theological
 Seminary
Fort Worth, Texas

Gayle Carlton Felton
Duke University Divinity School
Durham, North Carolina

Joseph Fichtner, O.S.C.
Crosier Community
Phoenix, Arizona

James F. Findlay
University of Rhode Island
Kingston, Rhode Island

David C. Ford
St. Tikhon's Orthodox Seminary
South Canaan, Pennsylvania

Robert V. Friedenberg
Miami (Ohio) University
Hamilton, Ohio

Robert Mikio Fukada
Doshisha University School of Theology
Kyoto, Japan

Reginald H. Fuller
Virginia Theological Seminary
Alexandria, Virginia

Beverly Roberts Gaventa
Princeton Theological Seminary
Princeton, New Jersey

Carol V. R. George
Hobart & William Smith Colleges
Geneva, New York

Peter J. Gomes
Memorial Church
Harvard University
Cambridge, Massachusetts

Catherine Gunsalus González
Columbia Theological Seminary
Decatur, Georgia

Justo L. González
Atlanta, Georgia

David M. Greenhaw
Lancaster Theological Seminary
Lancaster, Pennsylvania

Gracia Grindal
Luther Northwestern Theological
 Seminary
Saint Paul, Minnesota

Eric W. Gritsch
Lutheran Theological Seminary
Gettysburg, Pennsylvania

Nancy Lammers Gross
Eastern Baptist Theological Seminary
Wynnewood, Pennsylvania

Paul W. F. Harms
Trinity Lutheran Seminary
Columbus, Ohio

George W. Harper
Alliance Biblical Seminary
Manila
Republic of the Philippines

Stanley M. Hauerwas
Duke University Divinity School
Durham, North Carolina

Richard B. Hays
Duke University Divinity School
Durham, North Carolina

Susan K. Hedahl
Lutheran Theological Seminary
Gettysburg, Pennsylvania

Richard P. Heitzenrater
Duke University Divinity School
Durham, North Carolina

Jan Hermelink
Martin-Luther University
Halle, Germany

William Hethcock
School of Theology
University of the South
Sewanee, Tennessee

Ann I. Hoch
Duke University Divinity School
Durham, North Carolina

Lucy Hogan
Wesley Theological Seminary
Washington, D.C.

Arthur G. Holder
Church Divinity School of the Pacific
Berkeley, California

Robert G. Hughes
Lutheran Theological Seminary
Philadelphia, Pennsylvania

Willie James Jennings
Duke University Divinity School
Durham, North Carolina

Joseph R. Jeter, Jr.
Brite Divinity School
Texas Christian University
Fort Worth, Texas

L. Gregory Jones
Loyola College
Baltimore, Maryland

John L. Kater, Jr.
Church Divinity School of the Pacific
Berkeley, California

Tsuneaki Kato
Evangelical Church of Japan
Kamakura, Japan

John Killinger
Beeson Divinity School
Samford University
Birmingham, Alabama

William McGuire King
Albright College
Reading, Pennsylvania

Jack Dean Kingsbury
Union Theological Seminary in Virginia
Richmond, Virginia

C. Benton Kline, Jr.
Columbia Theological Seminary
Decatur, Georgia

Gary Kowalski
First Unitarian Universalist Society of
   Burlington
Burlington, Vermont

James N. Lapsley
Sun City, Arizona

George Lawless
Augustinianum
Istituto Patristico
Rome, Italy

William B. Lawrence
Duke University Divinity School
Durham, North Carolina

John H. Leith
Union Theological Seminary in Virginia
Richmond, Virginia

Ralph L. Lewis
Asbury Theological Seminary
Wilmore, Kentucky

Richard Lischer
Duke University Divinity School
Durham, North Carolina

Hugh Litchfield
North American Baptist Seminary
Sioux Falls, South Dakota

D. Stephen Long
Duke University Divinity School
Durham, North Carolina

Thomas G. Long
Princeton Theological Seminary
Princeton, New Jersey